THE 10™

Most Destructive Ecosystem Invaders

Lisa Cheung

Series Editor
Jeffrey D. Wilhelm

Much thought, debate, and research went into choosing and ranking the 10 items in each book in this series. We realize that everyone has his or her own opinion of what is most significant, revolutionary, amazing, deadly, and so on. As you read, you may agree with our choices, or you may be surprised — and that's the way it should be!

an imprint of
SCHOLASTIC
www.scholastic.com/librarypublishing

A Rubicon book published in association with Scholastic Inc.

Ru'bĭcon © 2008 Rubicon Publishing Inc.
www.rubiconpublishing.com

Associate Publishers: Kim Koh, Miriam Bardswich
Project Editor: Amy Land
Editor: Joyce Thian
Creative Director: Jennifer Drew
Project Manager/Designer: Jeanette MacLean
Graphic Designer: Brandon Köpke

The publisher gratefully acknowledges the following for permission to reprint copyrighted material in this book.

Every reasonable effort has been made to trace the owners of copyrighted material and to make due acknowledgment. Any errors or omissions drawn to our attention will be gladly rectified in future editions.

"Dance of Death" (excerpt) from "You can call him 'cute' or you can call him 'hungry'" by Richard Conniff. From *Smithsonian*, February 1997. Reprinted by permission of the author, from the book *Every Creeping Thing* (Holt).

"New species of crab threatens west coast fish habitat" from CBC News, August 1, 1999. Courtesy of CBC.ca.

Cover image: Chinese mitten crab–Louie Pslhoyos/Science Faction/Getty Images

Library and Archives Canada Cataloguing in Publication

Cheung, Lisa
    The 10 most destructive ecosystem invaders / Lisa Cheung.

Includes index.
ISBN: 978-1-55448-489-8

1. Readers (Elementary). 2. Readers — Biotic communities.
I. Title. II. Title: Ten most destructive ecosystem invaders.

PE1117.C54 2007   428.6   C2007-906855-3

1 2 3 4 5 6 7 8 9 10   10   17 16 15 14 13 12 11 10 09 08

Printed in Singapore

Contents

18

22

38

GET OUT!

Have you ever watched a competition where one team or side was much stronger, faster, or more skillful than its rivals? What's the usual outcome when one group of competitors has such great advantages?

In reality, very similar competitions are taking place in ecosystems around the world. Ecosystems develop a natural balance of native plants and animals over time. When invasive species enter an ecosystem, they can upset this balance, and life can suddenly become much harder for everyone. Because invasive species aren't held in check by predators or competitors that they faced in their homelands, they can spread rapidly and aggressively. As a result, invaders can displace native species, disrupt ecosystems, and even harm human populations.

ecosystems: *plants and animals together with their environment*
native: *originally living in a certain place*

Of course, some newly introduced species have little or no impact on their new habitats. Some may even have a positive effect. But then there are others that leave a trail of destruction wherever they go.

For this book, we chose what we thought are the 10 most destructive ecosystem invaders in the world. Then we ranked the ecosystem invaders according to these criteria: Do they take over the area? How quickly do they multiply and spread? Are they hard to keep in check? How do they outcompete native species? How do they change their surrounding environment? Do they pose a threat to public health? What sort of damage do they cause to human property or industries?

Before we go on to meet some of the worst ecosystem invaders the world has seen, ask yourself …

introduced: *brought to a new environment*
outcompete: *overpower or defeat another species in the competition for space, food, or other resources*

WHAT MAKES AN ECOSYSTEM INVADER TRULY DESTRUCTIVE?

Zebra mussels often attach themselves to each other, forming dense clusters up to 12 inches thick.

AKA: *Dreissena polymorpha* (Dree-eye-see-nay pol-lee-mor-fay)

WHAT IT IS: A marine animal called a mollusk

MEANS OF INVASION: Unknowingly transported by a transatlantic ship

IMPACT: Competes with native species for food; completely covers any underwater surfaces

At first glance, the zebra mussel seems like a harmless creature. It doesn't bite or sting. It doesn't even move around very much. So how did it make it onto everyone's most wanted list?

Unfortunately, when zebra mussels invade an area outside their home territory, they become a menace. Once they settle in, they will take over their new environment. Like cockroaches, zebra mussels reproduce rapidly and in large numbers. They crowd together in huge, nearly immovable clusters. They are also efficient eaters and so they easily beat their competition when it comes to finding food. As if all that wasn't bad enough, a zebra mussel infestation can damage just about anything in the water.

Today, it seems as if nothing can keep the zebra mussel invasion in check. They are gradually spreading into more and more new areas. In fact, scientists believe that once zebra mussels become established in a body of water, they are impossible to eradicate. Many chemicals can kill zebra mussels. But zebra mussels are so tolerant and tough that everything in the water would have to be poisoned to destroy them. Do we have any chance against these tiny aquatic invaders?

infestation: *state of being overrun by a species*
established: *well adjusted and able to thrive and persist*
eradicate: *destroy; wipe out*

ZEBRA MUSSEL

ON THE MOVE

The zebra mussel is native to the Black and Caspian seas in southeastern Europe. By the 1800s, it had spread west across Europe. In the late 1980s, it arrived in North America. Scientists believe a cargo ship traveling from the Black Sea to the Great Lakes unknowingly brought over the first zebra mussels. By the early 1990s, zebra mussels had been found in all the Great Lakes. From there, they have spread into many of the region's waterways and lakes.

Quick Fact

The early, larval form of the zebra mussel floats freely in water. The larvae are tiny and can easily be carried away by currents or picked up by unsuspecting ships loading water as ballast.

ballast: *heavy material carried by a ship to keep it stable*

WHAT'S FOR DINNER?

A filter feeder, the zebra mussel strains its food from the water. It mainly feeds on tiny, free-floating plants and animals called plankton. As an invader, it competes with native fish and mussels that also eat plankton. A large zebra mussel population can filter great volumes of water a day, quickly depleting the food resources that native species need to survive.

waterways: *bodies of water through which ships can travel, such as rivers, canals, and channels*

depleting: *using up*

? What kind of chain reaction is set off by the invasive zebra mussel as it outcompetes native species for plankton?

INVASIVE MENACE

Zebra mussels colonize all types of surfaces. A large colony of zebra mussels clustered together can completely cover rocks and seabeds. Zebra mussels can also clog water pipes and even suffocate native mussels and clams. They attach firmly to surfaces and are very hard to remove. Power stations, steel plants, water treatment facilities, and water suppliers spend billions of dollars every year removing zebra mussel colonies from their pipes.

As a zebra mussel colony filters for food, the infested body of water rapidly becomes clearer. This allows sunlight to shine deeper into the water. As a result, aquatic plants will grow in number and size, and light-sensitive fish may move to deeper waters.

colonize: *settle in and occupy or take over*

A zebra mussel larva can survive for a month with little or no food. As an adult, it can stay alive for a week or more out of water.

10   **9**   **8**

Invasive Species 101

What can scientists do about invasive species? Read this fact chart to find out, and then check out the report below on what can be done about the zebra mussel invasion.

Prevention	Stop the invasive species from entering in the first place.
Early identification and rapid response	Look for areas where the invasive species might invade or has already begun to do so. Quickly destroy it before it settles in.
Control	If the invasive species cannot be uprooted and destroyed, keep it from spreading further.
Restoration	Re-create the native ecosystem if possible. Try to bring it back to an earlier or original state.

Zebra mussels can clog pipes entirely.

Damage Control

The zebra mussel arrived in North America in the late 1980s. Since then, it has become firmly established, spreading over time to more and more areas.

Scientists believe it's now impossible to eradicate the zebra mussel. However, even though we can't remove these mussels from a lake or river, we can prevent their spread into non-infested waters.

Boaters should look out for and remove any zebra mussels that have attached to boat hulls, motors, trailers, or anchors. Diving equipment used in infested waters should be cleaned. Ships traveling to non-infested areas must not dump ballast water that was loaded in an infested area.

The Expert Says...

" I don't mean to demonize the zebra mussel as a species. It's just doing its job. It's a filterer. The key point here is it's completely beyond the control of management agencies or science. "

— Hugh MacIsaac, biology professor, University of Windsor, Ontario, Canada

Take Note

The zebra mussel clings to the #10 spot. By filtering water for food and colonizing all surfaces it can find, the zebra mussel is an ecological threat and a physical nuisance. It multiples rapidly and is almost impossible to destroy.
• Imagine that you're leading a project to stop the zebra mussel invasion in North America. Who would you seek help and cooperation from, and why?

5   4   3   2   1

The American comb jelly is small and has no stingers. Its body is covered with wart-like bumps.

AMERICAN COMB JELLY–© HERB SEGARS/MAXXIMAGES.COM

MB JELLY

AKA: *Mnemiopsis leidyi* (Nee-mee-op-sis lee-dee-eye)

WHAT IS IT? A marine animal called a ctenophore (ten-uh-fore)

MEANS OF INVASION: Unknowingly transported by a transatlantic ship

IMPACT: Devours animal plankton, including fish eggs and other larvae; changes the conditions of its surroundings

The American comb jelly's nicknames say it all for this aquatic invader. Some people call it "the blob that ate the Black Sea." Others call it simply "the monster."

The problem with this comb jelly is that it's a voracious predator. It's an eating machine! It will devour almost anything in its path. It eats and eats ... and then eats some more! Sometimes, it doesn't even know when to stop. When it has eaten too much, it simply vomits excess food as a ball of mucus. When it can't find any food at all to eat, it can survive for up to three weeks by reducing its body size. Finally, if all this isn't bad enough, this slimy monster reproduces at an alarming rate.

The American comb jelly's eating habits have been blamed for ruining ecosystems and destroying fisheries in the areas it has invaded.

Often considered North America's revenge for the zebra mussel, the comb jelly takes the #9 spot on our list ...

---

voracious: *having a huge appetite*
predator: *something that hunts or kills others for food*

AMERICAN COMB JELLY

ON THE MOVE

The American comb jelly is native to the eastern coasts of North and South America. In the early 1980s, ships carrying ballast water from this region transported the comb jelly to a port in the Black Sea. It infested that area quickly and soon spread to the nearby Sea of Azov. By the 1990s, it had spread to the Caspian and Mediterranean seas and connected waterways.

Quick Fact

Not all stowaway organisms picked up in ballast water survive a trip across the ocean. In a ballast tank, changes in temperature and lack of food and light will kill many of these organisms.

The body of the American comb jelly has rows of hair-like cilia (sill-ee-uh). These cilia beat back and forth to help the comb jelly swim.

WHAT'S FOR DINNER?

The American comb jelly feeds by slowly swimming around. This pumps water over the mucus-covered parts of its body that trap food. The American comb jelly eats animal plankton (or "zooplankton"), including fish eggs and other larvae. It can eat many times its body weight. Sometimes it will even keep eating after its stomach is full. This comb jelly is such a voracious predator that it can almost completely eliminate the zooplankton population of an area it invades.

INVASIVE MENACE

This comb jelly destroys ecosystems. When it invades an area where it has no natural predator, it spreads rapidly. It then breaks the food web. Native fish stocks in the Black, Azov, and Caspian seas collapsed after the introduction of the comb jelly. Not only did native species suffer, but the fisheries in these areas also sustained major losses.

food web: *system of food chains in an ecosystem that depend upon one another*

Quick Fact

In 2004, scientists decided to introduce the *Beroe ovata* to the Caspian Sea. Because this comb jelly eats only other comb jellies, scientists hoped it would wipe out the American comb jelly. This would allow the zooplankton population to recover.

? What factors do you think scientists consider before introducing a non-native predator to combat an invasive species?

ECOSYSTEM DESTROYE

When the American comb jelly invaded the Black Sea, it was met with very few natural predators. One thing soon led to another as the invader spread quickly in its new home. Read this report to find out exactly what happened ...

The Black Sea has a natural shortage c oxygen and has always had problems wit algae. Algae cover the water surface. The can be a problem because they use up oxyger leaving very little for other sea life. On the othe hand, algae also shade beds of sea grass These beds produce oxygen and act as a hom for fish, crustaceans, and sponges.

The zooplankton population in the Black Se plays a big role in this ecosystem's delicat balancing act. Zooplankton feed on the alga that would otherwise grow out of control.

When the American comb jelly arrived in th Black Sea, it began to feed on zooplankton. It at so much, so quickly, that it virtually eliminate the zooplankton population in the sea.

With less and less zooplankton around, alga began to grow out of control. As a result, oxyge levels went down.

The American comb jelly completely changed it surrounding environment. Before long, it made u more than 90 percent of all biomass present i the Black Sea.

algae: *plants or plant-like organisms that grow mostly in water*
biomass: *total amount of living material in a habitat*

A close-up of an American comb jelly eating zooplankton

Quick Fact

The American comb jelly is a hermaphrodite (her-muh-fro-dyte). This means it has both male and female reproductive organs. It can fertilize itself, producing thousands of eggs per day.

The Expert Says...

" One of the more devastating alien invasions in the past 20 years has been the arrival of a gelatinous American import [the American comb jelly] in the Black Sea and adjacent waterways. "

— Janet Raloff, senior editor, *Science News*

gelatinous: *jelly-like*
adjacent: *lying next to or near*

Take Note

The American comb jelly takes the #9 spot. When it has no natural predators, it can destroy an ecosystem. It eats excessively, changes its surroundings, and reproduces at an alarming rate.
• Compare and contrast the effects of the American comb jelly and the zebra mussel on the areas they invade.

5   4   3   2   1

The northern Pacific sea star can grow up to 20 inches wide. The upturned tips of its five arms help distinguish it from other starfish species.

CIFIC SEA STAR

AKA: *Asterias amurensis* (As-teh-ree-as ah-myur-en-sis)

WHAT IT IS: A marine animal called a starfish

MEANS OF INVASION: Transported unknowingly by a transpacific ship

IMPACT: Preys on a variety of native species; rapidly establishes large populations in new areas

Scientists in Australia are keeping a close eye on the northern Pacific sea star. Ever since it arrived Down Under, it has been roaming the waters in search of food. It will eat anything it can get its arms on. Worse yet, this sea star has a way of making sure its prey can't hide from it.

The northern Pacific sea star leaves a trail of destruction wherever it goes. In infested areas, people have removed tens of thousands of these sea stars from the water in an attempt to eradicate it. Not only can these attempts backfire, but they do little to end the infestation. There are just too many of the sea stars, and they multiply very quickly. Even in its native waters, the northern Pacific sea star is a major pest.

The northern Pacific sea star also has an amazing ability that helps it survive most attacks …

NORTHERN PACIFIC SEA STAR

ON THE MOVE

The northern Pacific sea star is native to the coasts of northeastern Asia. It is also found in the northern Pacific waters off North America. In the mid-1980s, it was introduced to southeastern Australia. Scientists believe it was brought to a port in Tasmania, Australia, in the ballast water of a ship from Japan.

WHAT'S FOR DINNER?

The northern Pacific sea star can detect food from far away and will even dig to get to buried prey. It's an opportunistic predator, so it will feed on whatever it can find. It prefers shellfish but will also eat worms, sea urchins, and other species of sea stars. If there's nothing else to feed on, the northern Pacific sea star will eat members of its own species. Scientists have even seen it eating dead fish and fish waste.

opportunistic: *taking advantage of circumstances for self-benefit*

INVASIVE MENACE

The northern Pacific sea star is a serious threat to coastal ecosystems. By eating a wide range of native marine animals, it greatly alters the food web of an area.

In Australia, the northern Pacific sea star affects shellfish, scallop, and oyster farms. Outbreaks cost marine industries millions of dollars every year in lost profits — the sea star devours the marine animals that fisheries depend on.

outbreaks: *sudden increases in numbers of a harmful organism within an area*

Quick Fact

The northern Pacific sea star can pry open a shellfish, squeeze its stomach through the opening, and inject digestive juices into the shellfish to weaken it. The shellfish will then open up completely, allowing the northern Pacific sea star to eat it.

Quick Fact

Even in Japan, which is part of its native range, the northern Pacific sea star is a major pest. Populations routinely reach plague proportions for two to three years before rapidly declining.

The northern Pacific sea star prefers to live in shallow, sheltered areas.

SURVIVOR!

The northern Pacific sea star can replace a lost or damaged body part by forming new tissue. This ability is called regeneration. Find out more in this fact chart.

★ In fact, all starfish can regenerate lost or damaged arms. However, most starfish can only do this if the central part of their body is still in one piece. But the northern Pacific sea star can regenerate itself entirely even if just a piece of the central part of its body remains.

★ Regeneration is a slow process. It can take up to a year for a sea star's regenerating arm to grow to its usual length.

★ The northern Pacific sea star's regeneration ability makes it hard to destroy. In the late 1990s, people in Tasmania, Australia, worked together to try to remove sea stars from their coastal waters. Unfortunately, they cut up the sea stars and threw them back into the water. Many of these cut-up sea stars regenerated, becoming multiple new sea stars, which made the infestation even worse.

Marine biologists in Australia have led efforts to try to gather as many sea stars as possible.

Quick Fact

The female northern Pacific sea star can produce between 10 and 25 million eggs per year. Once the eggs are fertilized, they develop into drifting larvae. They remain as larvae for up to 120 days before becoming juvenile sea stars.

? How do you think this drifting period increases the sea star's ability to invade new environments?

The Expert Says...

" [The northern Pacific sea star has] all the characteristics that make it an ideal invader and pest. "

— Caroline Sutton, marine biologist, CSIRO Marine and Atmospheric Research

Take Note

The northern Pacific sea star ranks #8 on our list. It is an opportunistic predator, which makes it even worse than the American comb jelly. On top of that, this sea star can regenerate itself and reproduce by the millions.

• Scientists decided to combat the American comb jelly invasion in Europe by bringing in a non-native predator. Do you think it would be wise to do the same with the northern Pacific sea star invasion in Australia? Why or why not?

5   4   3   2   1

(7) STOAT

The stoat has a long, thin body and neck, a pointed head, small ears, short arms and legs, and a black-tipped tail. It grows to around 12 – 16 inches long. This stoat is raiding a bird's nest.

AKA: *Mustela erminea* (Mus-tuh-luh er-min-ee-uh)

WHAT IT IS: A mammal; a type of weasel

MEANS OF INVASION: Introduced on purpose

IMPACT: Preys on small mammals and native bird species, driving many to extinction

With such an adorable little face, the stoat looks more like a cuddly pet than the natural born killer it is. Don't be fooled — this little weasel is a smart, versatile, and fearless predator.

A stoat on the prowl will swiftly hunt its prey down, whether its target is on the ground or in a tree. Most small mammals and birds are no match for the stoat. Normal running, ducking, hiding, or climbing escapes will not work against this predator. The stoat will kill anything it can eat and then some. Finally, it has been known to take over the burrows of animals it finishes off!

The stoat's fearsome ways wouldn't be such a concern to scientists today had it not been for a grave mistake that was made more than 100 years ago.

burrows: *holes or tunnels dug in the ground by a small animal, used as a home or hideout*

STOAT

ON THE MOVE

The stoat is native to the northern regions of North America, Europe, and Asia. Around the mid-1880s, it was introduced to New Zealand. It was intentionally brought in to help control the growing populations of rabbits and pest rodents. The stoat population grew rapidly and, within a few years, began to invade and colonize New Zealand's main and nearby islands.

WHAT'S FOR DINNER?

The stoat is an opportunistic carnivore. It will eat small mammals, birds, eggs, fish, reptiles, and even garbage. It does not hesitate to go after larger animals. If it's possible, the stoat will often kill more than it can eat. Any extras are stored for later.

This stoat is eating a mouse.

INVASIVE MENACE

Instead of helping New Zealand with its rabbit and rodent problems, the stoat became a pest itself. It began to kill many of the other readily available native species in the country. According to some studies, the stoat is responsible for killing up to 60 percent of all kiwi chicks on New Zealand's North Island. It is also linked to the extinction or sudden population drop of 13 native bird species in the country.

Quick Fact

The stoat can really move! Leaping and running, it can reach speeds of up to 18 mph. With sharp claws, it is also skilled at climbing trees. Last but not least, it's also a good swimmer!

DANCE OF DEATH

An article from *Smithsonian* magazine
By Richard Conniff, February 1997

Suddenly, the stoat appeared, bounding zigzag across the grass to a drainage ditch. ... She stood on her hind legs, brown and sleek, showing her creamy white underbelly. Her long snake-like head pivoted from side to side, frantically scanning the grass to see if she'd stirred up any movement. She leaned forward, as if about to dart at something, then leaped right, and left, and disappeared again, popping up a moment later, 10 yards away. ...

She appeared to be both manic and systematic, demented and yet thorough, qualities that have also been ascribed to the reputed "dance of death," in which the weasel spins and somersaults like a lunatic, causing birds to gawk and draw close. At the height of the dance, the weasel, suddenly sane, darts out and puts a death lock on the neck of the nearest member of the audience. ...

The stoat may not have enough strength in its upper jaw to penetrate the rabbit's skull and meet the lower canines coming up from the throat, but the rabbit, squealing pitifully, usually dies anyway, of fright.

pivoted: *turned; twirled*
manic: *overexcited*
penetrate: *stab; break into*

? What makes the stoat such a fearsome predator and invasive species?

Quick Fact
The stoat is territorial — it doesn't like having other stoats near its home. (The only exception is during mating season.) Within its territory, the stoat often makes use of several burrows, most of which originally belonged to other animals that were killed by the stoat.

? Why do you think certain animals are territorial?

The government of New Zealand spends millions of dollars a year researching how to control the stoat invasion. It described the stoat as "public enemy number one" for the country's native birds.

The Expert Says...
"Stoats are quick and clever. ... In critical areas, just one stoat in the wrong place can do a lot of damage."

— Dr. Cheryl O'Connor,
   Pest Control and Wildlife
   Toxicology team leader,
   Landcare Research,
   New Zealand

Take Note
The stoat takes the #7 spot. It's a fearsome predator. It can quickly spread to new areas, traveling over land and water in search of prey. Even worse, the stoat will kill more animals than it can eat in order to stockpile for the future.
• Besides the stoat, other non-native species of animals and plants have been introduced to New Zealand. Find out what they are and see whether they have become ecosystem pests, too.

CHERYL CONNOR–LAND CARE RESEARCH; ALL OTHER IMAGES–SHUTTERSTOCK, ISTOCKPHOTO

5   4   3   2   1

The giant African land snail has a distinctively large, shiny, cone-shaped shell. It can grow up to eight inches long and five inches wide.

N LAND SNAIL

AKA: *Achatina fulica* (Ah-kuh-tee-nuh full-ick-uh)

WHAT IT IS: A mollusk

MEANS OF INVASION: Smuggled in by individuals

IMPACT: Damages food crops and native plants; carries parasites and diseases

The giant African land snail is slow and has poor eyesight. But it doesn't let these factors stop it from getting several square meals a day. In fact, this large, voracious snail is considered one of the worst pests in tropical areas because of its relentless eating!

The giant African land snail is hard to get rid of once it has infested an area. Immediate action needs to be taken at the first sign of invasion; otherwise this snail is here to stay. Scientists in infested areas have tried everything — some collect as many snails as they can by hand, others leave poisons around, and still others burn the pests alive with flamethrowers! What will they think of next?

relentless: *steady and persistent*

GIANT AFRICAN LAND SNAIL

ON THE MOVE

The giant African land snail is native to eastern Africa. Around the mid-19th century, it was introduced to various islands in the Indian Ocean. Within decades, it spread to nearby parts of Asia and then to islands in the southern Pacific Ocean. In the 1980s, researchers brought the snail over from Asia to South America, where it quickly became established. Recently, it reached the Caribbean.

? Some countries, such as Britain, allow the giant African land snail to be kept as pets. Others, such as the United States, ban the snail from even entering the country. Why do you think different countries have different rules concerning this snail?

WHAT'S FOR DINNER?

The giant African land snail is a herbivore. It feeds on more than 500 different plants and crops, including peanuts, beans, peas, cucumbers, and melons. It will even eat tree bark, rotten or decaying vegetation, animal feces, and the paint and stucco on the sides of houses. This snail is also known to eat sand, small stones, and concrete. It easily outcompetes native snails for food resources in the area it infests.

Sunshine is fatal for the giant African land snail. It buries itself underground during the day and only feeds at night.

INVASIVE MENACE

The giant African land snail can munch its way through large quantities of crops and native plants. In Florida, officials estimated that an outbreak of this snail in 1969 would have cost the state $11 million if it hadn't been stopped. Just by being around, this snail can change an invaded area's food web — it's a new food source for native predators. It can also carry parasites that are harmful to humans who handle the snails or eat them raw or undercooked. Even after it dies, this snail can still affect the environment. The decaying body of a giant African land snail releases a bad stench. A leftover shell, which is made of a substance called calcium carbonate, will reduce the acid levels in the surrounding soil. This harms plants that would grow better in acidic soil.

parasites: *organisms that live off other organisms*

When the weather becomes cold or dry, the giant African land snail can adapt by sealing itself in its shell. This way it won't lose any water and can wait for the weather to become hotter and more humid.

10   7   **6**

SNAIL TALES

The reports below are just two pieces of the puzzle when it comes to how the worldwide giant African land snail invasion began ...

FAST FOOD

Some researchers say that during World War II, giant African land snails were brought to islands in the southern Pacific Ocean to be food reserves for soldiers. Unfortunately, some of the snails escaped into the wild. A predator snail was then brought in to combat the invasion. But the predator snail ended up going after a native snail in the area instead of the giant African snail. The native snail eventually became extinct.

FROM PET TO PEST

In 1966, a young boy smuggled some giant African land snails back home to Florida after a vacation in Hawaii. He wanted to keep the snails as pets but ended up releasing them. Over the next seven years, more than 18,000 snails and countless eggs were found. It took officials 10 years and several quarantines, snail hunts, and chemical snail exterminations to put an end to the Florida infestation. The total cost: roughly $1 million.

quarantines: *limiting or preventing the movements of persons or goods to keep pests from spreading*

Quick Fact

The giant African land snail's lifespan ranges from five to nine years. Every year, it can produce hundreds of eggs. About 90 percent of these eggs hatch, developing into adults in just four months.

The Expert Says...

" The more insidious conservation problem [with giant African land snails] is that they tempt agricultural officials to initiate a number of putative biological control measures. "

— Robert H. Cowie, Department of Natural Sciences, Bishop Museum

insidious: *gradually becoming harmful*
putative: *assumed to be true without evidence*

Take Note

The giant African land snail crawls into the #6 spot. Its movements may be slow, but its appetite for all sorts of plants and crops can be devastating. It reproduces rapidly, so a local invasion can easily turn into a widespread infestation. Finally, this snail carries parasites that can directly harm humans!

• Why and how should local community members take action to manage invasive species?

5   4   3   2   1

The female gypsy moth lays her eggs directly on tree trunks, as seen here.

AKA: *Lymantria dispar* (Ly-mon-tree-uh dis-per)

WHAT IT IS: An insect

MEANS OF INVASION: Imported by an individual and then released unintentionally

IMPACT: Damages trees by eating all their leaves

It's here, it's hairy, and it's hungry! As a young caterpillar, the gypsy moth is a ravenous little pest. You will be amazed at how much and how quickly it eats.

The gypsy moth caterpillar can hang from a tree on a silk thread. When the wind blows, the caterpillar can then drift for many miles to a new location. This is known as "ballooning" and allows the gypsy moth to spread to other areas.

An invasion of this insect can only get worse over time. The female gypsy moth reproduces only once in her lifetime. But she can lay a mass of up to 1,000 eggs at one time! Most importantly, she will lay her eggs on almost anything outdoors, from tree trunks to rocks to cars to fences. After one winter season, the eggs hatch and another invasion begins.

ravenous: *extremely hungry; voracious*

GYPSY MOTH

ON THE MOVE

The gypsy moth is native to Europe and Asia. In the late 1860s, it was introduced to eastern North America. A researcher imported some egg masses and when they hatched, some of the caterpillars escaped into the wild. By the early 1880s, the first outbreaks of gypsy moths had begun to appear. This moth now infests many regions in eastern North America, including northeastern United States and eastern Canada.

When the gypsy moth caterpillar matures, it spins a cocoon where it lives for two weeks before changing into an adult moth.

WHAT'S FOR DINNER?

The gypsy moth caterpillar isn't fussy about what it eats. It will feed on the leaves of a wide range of trees, shrubs, and vines. However, it does prefer broad-leaved trees, such as red and white oak, poplar, and white birch. Scientists estimate that a gypsy moth caterpillar can eat about one square yard of leaves per day.

INVASIVE MENACE

A large population of gypsy moth caterpillars can completely strip all the leaves from surrounding trees and shrubs. Over time, these trees may die. A gypsy moth outbreak can affect the natural diversity and survival of native insects, birds, and other animals. These species suffer when the loss of healthy host trees leads to less shelter and fewer food resources.

The gypsy moth caterpillar's hairs can cause people to have allergic reactions ranging from rashes and welts to shortness of breath.

diversity: *variety; range*

? Stripping a tree of its leaves is called defoliation. Repeated defoliation weakens trees, leading to disease, other infestations, and death. Why do you think the loss of its leaves is so damaging to a tree?

The hairy gypsy moth caterpillar is easy to spot. Lining its back are five pairs of blue dots followed by six pairs of red dots.

The Expert Says...

" The gypsy moth is fully entrenched in the United States. We will never eradicate it. The goal now is to slow that natural spread. "

— Dr. Vic Mastro, Animal and Plant Health Inspection Service, U.S. Department of Agriculture

entrenched: *firmly fixed or established*

IN THE NEWS

Invasions of gypsy moth caterpillars continually made the news in 2007. Check out these newspaper clippings ...

THE MOTHS A-COMETH

The Hamilton Spectator, September 19, 2007

HAMILTON, ONTARIO — Hold onto your bug spray. Experts say next summer's infestation of gypsy moth caterpillars will be even worse than this year.

Gypsy moth caterpillars attack!

UPI NewsTrack, July 1, 2007

PHILADELPHIA — New Jersey and Pennsylvania are seeing their worst invasion of damaging gypsy moth caterpillars in nearly two decades ...

NIGHTMARE OF SQUIRMING VERMIN

Milwaukee Journal Sentinel, June 19, 2007

MILWAUKEE — The state Department of Natural Resources took unprecedented action and closed Rocky Arbor State Park near Wisconsin Dells on Monday to prevent the spread of a virulent gypsy moth outbreak.

unprecedented: *never done before*

GYPSY MOTH DAMAGE ON THE RISE

The New York Times, June 17, 2007

NEW YORK — A record number of trees are expected to fall victim to gypsy moth caterpillars this year, according to the New Jersey Department of Agriculture.

Take Note

The gypsy moth drifts into the #5 spot. Like the giant African land snail, the gypsy moth is also a herbivore with a big appetite. But an infestation of the gypsy moth can spread quickly and widely and threaten a wide range of trees and plants in North America.

• Compare the ways in which the gypsy moth and the giant African land snail can affect people's health.

5   **4**   **3**   **2**   **1**

When the Chinese mitten crab stretches out its legs, it can easily measure over 11 inches long.

TEN CRAB

AKA: *Eriocheir sinensis* (Eh-ree-oh-keer si-nen-sis)

WHAT IT IS: A marine animal called a crustacean (crus-tay-shun)

MEANS OF INVASION: Transported unknowingly in ballast water; possibly smuggled in

IMPACT: Eats and outcompetes native species; causes lasting damage to surrounding environment; can carry a parasite that harms humans

The Chinese mitten crab's behavior causes serious damage. It can destroy its habitats. It can push endangered native species to the brink of extinction. And it can cost local industries millions of dollars in damage control every year.

That's not all. The Chinese mitten crab is very adaptable. It lives in water, but it can travel long distances on land. In fact, the Chinese mitten crab has been known to invade new areas by walking over dry land to nearby waterways. Researchers have tried to keep the Chinese mitten crab from migrating and spreading into non-infested areas, but not much has worked. They don't call this invasive pest the "migrating crab" for nothing! As well, the mitten crab thrives in a wide range of climates. It can even survive in polluted waters.

But there's more! The mitten crab multiplies and spreads at a shocking rate. A single female can produce up to one million eggs. These eggs hatch into freely floating larvae. Not only do these larvae spread easily through a body of water, but they also become young crabs in less than two months. No wonder scientists are worried about this monstrous crab …

adaptable: *able to adjust to new, different environments*
migrating: *moving from one place to another*

ON THE MOVE

The Chinese mitten crab is native to south-eastern Asia. It has been transported to many parts of the world in ballast water and possibly by smuggling. In the 1900s, it arrived in north-central Europe. For about 30 years, it spread quickly, establishing itself in many waterways in Europe and western Asia. Between the 1960s and 1980s, it was introduced to the mid-Atlantic coast and Great Lakes of North America. In the early 1990s, it was brought to the mid-Pacific coast of North America, where it is now firmly established.

Quick Fact

In China, mitten crabs have been known to migrate more than 900 miles along some rivers.

WHAT'S FOR DINNER?

The mitten crab is an opportunistic omnivore. When it's still young, it feeds on vegetation such as algae and aquatic plants. As it matures, it will feed on all sorts of small invertebrates, crustaceans, and fish.

omnivore: *organism that eats plants and animals*
invertebrates: *animals that don't have a backbone*

The Chinese mitten crab was named for its funny-looking claws, which are covered with a dense patch of soft, hairlike bristles.

INVASIVE MENACE

The Chinese mitten crab burrows deep into the banks of rivers and levees. As the land weakens from the holes, it erodes faster, sinks, and sometimes even collapses. Besides damaging the environment, the Chinese mitten crab easily outcompetes local insects and crayfish for plant food. It also preys on native invertebrates such as worms and clams, as well as crustaceans such as crayfish and shrimp.

An outbreak of Chinese mitten crabs greatly affects local industries. Fisheries suffer when the crabs infest fish-farm ponds, steal fish bait, damage fishing gear, and eat trapped fish. Power plants and water supply facilities spend millions of dollars removing the crabs when large numbers of them clog water pipes.

The Chinese mitten crab can also carry a parasite that is harmful to humans.

levees: *mounds of earth or stone built to keep rivers from overflowing*

Fact or fiction? Some people in Germany say Chinese mitten crabs wander the streets at night and even enter houses!

Quick Fact

In its native China and Korea, the Chinese mitten crab has been known to crawl out of waterways and invade rice fields. They will eat rice shoots and burrow into parts of the rice field.

10 9 8 6

NEW SPECIES OF CRAB THREATENS WEST COAST FISH HABITAT

An article from CBC News, August 1, 1999

British Columbia fisheries officials met this weekend with several U.S. [state] governments to discuss a new threat to the west coast fishery. A pesky crab species from China is causing a major dilemma for governments on both sides of the border.

The unwelcome, hairy-clawed guests may soon arrive in Canadian waters. "Mitten crabs" have already invaded the shores of California. Millions of them have clogged pipes and stolen food and habitat from other fish.

Dede Alpert, a [former California state] senator from San Diego, suggests Canadians be vigilant about the mitten crab. "If there's even one crab spotted, immediately take action," she warns.

Alpert said fisheries officials in California weren't initially aware of how quickly the mitten crabs could spread and cause trouble. "By the time we really got on this ... actually put some resources toward it, we just had literally millions on our hands."

California now outlaws the possession of live mitten crabs. Alpert recommends killing any crabs that might make their way north.

dilemma: *difficult situation*

> Researchers in Germany installed electrical screens to try to prevent Chinese mitten crabs from migrating and spreading into new areas. It didn't work. What else do you think could prevent or control a mitten crab invasion?

The Chinese mitten crab's burrowing habit is very destructive to its surrounding environment, as seen here.

> The Chinese mitten crab is catadromous (cuh-ta-druh-mus). It lives in fresh water but must move to salt water to reproduce. How do you think this affects its range?

The Expert Says...

" Don't be fooled by its cute name — this crab is not cute! Its wide diet, population explosions, and destructive burrowing habits make it a real cause for concern in the many places it has invaded. "

— Dr. Deborah Rudnick, senior scientist, Integral Consulting Inc., Maryland

Take Note

The Chinese mitten crab grabs the #4 spot. This crab can cause serious ecological, economic, and human health problems. It multiplies rapidly and migrates easily to new territory. It can also survive in a wide range of conditions.
• Which type of invasive species is worse: one that can travel long distances by itself, or one that can be transported unknowingly?

5   **4**   3   2   1

3 CANE TOAD

The large, poisonous cane toad can grow to 10 inches long and weigh up to 5.5 pounds.

AKA: *Bufo marinus* (Boo-foe mayr-ih-nus)

WHAT IT IS: An amphibian

MEANS OF INVASION: Deliberately imported

IMPACT: Eats native species and outcompetes them for food and shelter; highly toxic and harmful to local predators

Here we have yet another example of how experiments can go wrong. In the 1930s, the cane toad was deliberately introduced to different areas of the world. The goal was to control beetle populations that were destroying cash crops. But the experiment failed miserably. As the world soon discovered, the cane toad couldn't really help combat the pest beetles. That's because this toad is a ground-dwelling predator! Unable to jump very high, it seldom feeds on beetles, which tend to inhabit high places.

To make things worse, this toad was very aggressive. It became an even more destructive pest than the beetles. And the cane toad isn't any ordinary toad — it can stop its predators in their tracks!

cash crops: *plants grown for profit*

CANE TOAD

ON THE MOVE

The cane toad is native to southern Texas, parts of Central America, and the Amazon basin in South America. Since the 1930s, it has been introduced to much of the Caribbean, islands in the mid-Pacific, parts of southeastern Asia, and Australia.

Quick Fact

The cane toad has spread over large areas of Australia on its own. It can hop to a new area by itself or be transported by trucks carrying cargo.

WHAT'S FOR DINNER?

This toad is an opportunistic omnivore — it will eat anything that fits in its mouth. It feeds mostly on insects but also preys on snails, other toads, frogs, tadpoles, snakes, and small lizards. It will even feed on small rodents. Finally, it has been known to eat pet food, garbage, dead animals, and feces. The cane toad will completely gorge itself when there's lots of food available.

gorge: *eat a very large amount*

Quick Fact

A large female cane toad can lay 8,000 to 30,000 eggs in a single spawning. The eggs hatch in two to seven days, and the tadpoles mature after about four to eight weeks.

This lawn in Australia is covered in cane toads during an outbreak.

INVASIVE MENACE

The cane toad outcompetes native species for food, shelter, and breeding sites. It reproduces in high numbers and spreads quickly. It's also poisonous as an egg, tadpole, and adult. Native species in invaded areas that haven't learned to avoid the cane toad's venom can easily be poisoned. Humans and household pets can be harmed, too. The cane toad can also carry diseases harmful to native frogs and fishes.

Small frogs are just some of the native species that cane toads prey on.

DO NOT DISTURB!

Have a look at this step-by-step account of how the cane toad responds to a threat or an attack …

Venom Glands

Venom Glands

! First, the cane toad inflates its lungs. It lifts its body off the ground and turns around so that its venom glands face the predator.

! The cane toad's venom either oozes or sprays out in a fine mist.

! If the predator tries to eat the cane toad, the toad's venom will get into its mouth. The toxins are then absorbed by tissues in the predator's mouth.

! If the predator eats the cane toad, it will end up eating venom that's still oozing from the toad's glands. As well, the toad's muscles, bones, and organs all contain toxins!

! Signs of venom poisoning include excess salivation, twitching, vomiting, shallow breathing, and collapse of the hind limbs. Some predators may even die from heart failure.

Quick Fact

In Australia, many local predators have died eating or trying to eat the cane toad. These include birds, snakes, and wild dogs.

The Expert Says…

" The short-term impact is disaster. Large numbers of indigenous creatures are going to die, and I think it's fanciful to believe everything will recover and we'll all learn to live with cane toads. "

— Michael J. Tyler, amphibian specialist

indigenous: *native*
fanciful: *unrealistic; wishful thinking*

Take Note

The cane toad takes the #3 spot on our list. Even though it might not travel as far as the Chinese mitten crab, this toad roams both land and water. It outcompetes native species. It even harms larger native species with its venom.
• Compare the disastrous introductions of the stoat into New Zealand and the cane toad into Australia. What are the similarities and differences?

? Some experts argue it's too early to say whether the cane toad is causing long-term damage in invaded areas. Why do you think there are differing opinions on the impacts of invasive species?

5   4   **3**   2   1

The brown tree snake is long and slender, which allows it to hide easily in small spaces. The average brown tree snake is 3 – 4 feet long, but it has been known to grow up to 10 feet long!

SNAKE

AKA: *Boiga irregularis* (Boy-ja ear-reg-you-lar-is)

WHAT IT IS: A reptile

MEANS OF INVASION: Transported unknowingly by a military cargo ship

IMPACT: Preys on native species, driving many to extinction; invades human environments

Experts call the brown tree snake's invasion of Guam (Gwahm) a "classic horror story." Guam is a small island in the western Pacific Ocean. The brown tree snake arrived more than 50 years ago and has caused nothing but nightmares ever since. That's because the snake found its perfect new home. It met no natural predators and barely any competition for food or shelter. Before long, brown tree snakes had colonized the entire island. They have torn through Guam's fragile ecosystem.

Native species have become extinct. Parts of the island are overrun with snakes. Residents and tourists worry about their health and safety. What can be done?

fragile: *easily damaged or destroyed*

BROWN TREE SNAKE

ON THE MOVE

The brown tree snake is native to islands in the southern Pacific Ocean. Specifically, it's found in eastern Indonesia, the Solomon Islands, Papua New Guinea, and the northern and eastern coasts of Australia. During World War II, it was introduced to Guam. Researchers believe it was accidentally transported with cargo on a military ship. Within decades, the snake had become established on the island.

WHAT'S FOR DINNER?

This snake is a generalized predator — it will eat a wide variety of food. While still young, it feeds on small lizards, frogs, and bird and reptile eggs. As an adult, it prefers larger animals, including birds, bats, and even small pets. It can live for long periods of time without food.

generalized: *not limited to a specific behavior*

A brown tree snake eating a bird

Quick Fact

When the brown tree snake attacks, it wraps its body around its prey to keep it still. It then bites and injects poison into the animal. This kills the animal so that the brown tree snake can eat it.

The brown tree snake lives in uninhabited areas, such as forests, caves, and cliffs. But it will also live in human environments, including grassland, pasture, farmland, and deforested land.

? What are some of the chain-reaction effects that could result from the brown tree snake's continued infestation of Guam?

INVASIVE MENACE

Birds native to Guam aren't able to defend themselves against a predator like the brown tree snake. Before this snake's arrival, Guam had only one native snake species and it was blind! Today, most of Guam's native bird species are either nearing extinction or have already become extinct. Native lizards are next and even small mammals are becoming rarer. As a result, some of their native predators now resort to scavenging garbage and even stealing food from humans.

The brown tree snake is also highly adaptable. It's used to living next to humans and often invades human environments. Besides frightening most residents and tourists, it can harm young children with its mildly venomous bite. This snake also climbs up power lines, which leads to frequent short circuits and power outages.

SNAKES ON THE ISLAND: WHAT CAN BE DONE?

Q: Could a predator be brought in to feed on the snake population?

A: You would think so. But there's a risk that the predator will hunt other prey on the island. Another non-native predator in Guam could just damage its ecosystem even more.

Q: Is it possible to just trap the snakes?

A: Yes, and this is being done. But in certain areas of Guam, there may be anywhere from 12,000 to 30,000 brown tree snakes per square mile. This is one of the highest snake densities in the world. Besides, this snake usually comes out at night. It is a good climber and can crawl through small openings as well. It can avoid capture by staying in trees, dense vegetation, or other places that are hard to get to. In the end, trapping is only a short-term solution — it can only reduce small, local populations.

Q: How about using bait, such as fake or poisoned items?

A: This snake isn't easily fooled by bait. It won't eat something if it seems unreal, unnatural, or potentially harmful in any way. Besides, native birds, mammals, reptiles, and even household pets could be poisoned, too.

SNAKE EATING BIRD; SNAKE ON LEAF –©LIMT ELLIS/MINDEN PICTURES/GETTY IMAGES; SNAKE ON TREE–© MICHAEL & PATRICIA FOGDEN/CORBIS; ALL OTHER IMAGES–ISTOCKPHOTO

The Expert Says...

" [This invasion is] a demonstration of what human carelessness can do to a closed ecosystem and how *formidable* and frustrating the problem can become — not to mention how difficult it can be to eradicate this kind of problem once it is out of the bottle. "

— Cathleen Short, Assistant Director, Fisheries and Habitat Conservation, U.S. Fish and Wildlife Service

formidable: *fearsome or alarming; difficult to overcome*

? Do you know what a closed ecosystem is? Do some research to find out. How does this term apply to Guam?

Take Note

The brown tree snake takes the #2 spot. Since arriving in Guam, it has had a widespread impact on the island's ecosystem, economy, electrical systems, and public health. It has hunted or will hunt several native species to extinction. And once a species is gone, it's gone forever — this is a permanent change that can do vast damage to an ecosystem.

• Why do you think closed ecosystems suffer more from the introduction of an invasive species?

5 4 3 **2** 1

As an adult, the Asian long-horned beetle has a shiny, black body dotted with white spots. Its long, black antennae are ringed with white bands.

HORNED BEETLE

AKA: *Anoplophora glabripennis* (Ah-no-plo-for-uh glab-ree-penn-ess)

WHAT IT IS: An insect

MEANS OF INVASION: Transported in wooden crates on transatlantic cargo ships

IMPACT: Damages and kills trees

No tree is safe with the Asian long-horned beetle around. This wood-chomping threat is a quiet killer. But it has been setting off alarm bells across North America ever since it arrived.

An invasion of the Asian long-horned beetle can easily turn into a full-blown infestation. And if an infestation goes unnoticed or unchecked, there's no telling how much damage there will be. The female Asian long-horned beetle chews holes in the bark of a tree where she lays her eggs. Hidden inside the bark, the eggs hatch into larvae after 10 to 15 days. The larvae will chew farther into the tree before chewing their way back out once they mature. The Asian long-horned beetle will dig into and feed on almost any kind of tree, healthy or sick, young or old.

The only certain way to get rid of Asian long-horned beetles is to destroy the infested trees. Once a tree becomes host to this beetle, that usually ensures its death.

ASIAN LONG-HORNED BEETLE

? Asian long-horned beetles are often accidentally transported while hidden in firewood, lumber, or wooden crates. But they can also spread on their own by flying to new host trees nearby. How do you think this affects attempts to control this beetle invasion?

ON THE MOVE

The Asian long-horned beetle is native to eastern Asia, specifically China, Korea, and Japan. In the late 1980s, they were introduced to eastern North America. Within 10 years, infestations were being reported in the U.S. Northeast and Upper Midwest, as well as eastern and central Canada. Around the same time, the beetle was introduced to central Europe.

An Asian long-horned beetle larva

The female Asian long-horned beetle seals the holes where she lays her eggs with digested wood called "frass."

WHAT'S FOR DINNER?

Asian long-horned beetles will feed on a wide variety of hardwood trees. They target those with broad leaves. They prefer maple, elm, horse chestnut, ash, birch, poplar, and willow, to name a few. The larvae feed on a host tree's inner tissues — as they mature, they dig deep into the wood, creating tunnels as they feed. Adults feed on a host tree's bark and leaves.

INVASIVE MENACE

Asian long-horned beetles do their greatest damage as larvae. Their tunneling and feeding habits can weaken and kill a host tree. A medium-sized tree will die from an infestation in just two to four years. If these beetles spread over a large area, they can significantly damage forest ecosystems. Farms, parks, and even urban areas can be affected. When an infestation is discovered, officials usually have no choice but to completely destroy all the host trees.

The loss of thousands of trees in invaded areas has a severe impact on humans. Activities and industries that depend on host trees suffer. In Canada, reports say that $11 billion could be lost every year if these beetles continue to spread.

Quick Fact

Asian long-horned beetles cause damage in their native range, too. In one province in China, a severe infestation resulted in 50 million trees being cut down in just three years in the early 1990s.

10   9   8   7   6

To Kill a Long-Horned Beetle

Across North America, there is an ongoing fight to eradicate the Asian long-horned beetle. This list outlines just a few of the safety measures that are being taken to combat the beetle invasion ...

A rotary tree stump grinder

Quarantines

To prevent people from accidentally helping these beetles spread, infested areas are quarantined. If you live in a quarantined area, you can't cut down infested trees. You also can't use, throw away, or move any wood from the area without a special permit. In addition, you can't plant trees that the beetles are known to infest.

Destroying infested trees

All infested trees are removed and chipped by trained workers. The chips are then burned. The stumps of infested trees are ground to below the soil level.

Insecticide treatments

Scientists recently found an insecticide that might help kill the beetle. They're still testing this insecticide, which is sprayed directly on an infested tree. Because it's highly toxic, the insecticide would have to be used with caution.

Extensive surveys

After the very last host tree is destroyed, an infested area must be surveyed at least once per year for the next three to five years. This is to make sure that the infestation has been completely destroyed. Trees located near an infested area are also checked by trained workers.

? Only trained workers should check and remove infested trees. Why do you think this precaution is taken when it comes to combating the Asian long-horned beetle?

The Expert Says...

" Since they can't tell if individual trees are infested [with Asian long-horned beetle larvae], if a neighboring tree is infested, they have to assume that all the trees [in the area] are infested. "

— Gerry Wyatt, professor of biology, Queen's University, Ontario, Canada

Take Note

The Asian long-horned beetle comes in at #1! No matter where it goes, it leaves a trail of destruction. It can have a huge impact on the environment, native species, and humans. An infestation can destroy large areas of trees, whether in a forest, in a park, on a farm, or on a neighborhood street. This beetle also hides so well that it often isn't discovered until it is too late.

• Imagine you're an invasive species specialist. Of all the ecosystem invaders in this book, which would you pick to study, and why?

5   4   3   2   1

We Thought …

Here are the criteria we used in ranking our 10 most destructive ecosystem invaders.

The invader:
- Outcompetes native species
- Poses a threat to human health
- Multiplies rapidly
- Damages the surrounding environment
- Damages human property
- Is impossible to eradicate once established
- Causes the extinction of native species
- Spreads easily to new areas
- Can adapt to new environments

What Do You Think?

1. Do you agree with our ranking? If you don't, try ranking the invaders yourself. Justify your ranking with data from your own research and reasoning. You may refer to our criteria, or you may want to draw up your own list of criteria.

2. Here are three other invaders that we considered but in the end did not include in our top 10 list: the little fire ant, European green crab, and walking catfish.
   - Find out more about these invaders. Do you think they should have made our list? Give reasons for your response.
   - Are there other invaders that you think should have made our list? Explain your choices.

Index